DEAL CAS

KENT

Jonathan Coad
MA, FsA

Deal Castle was built by Henry VIII in the late 1530s in response to a threat of invasion by the Catholic powers of Europe. It was originally designed to guard the Kent coast and the Downs anchorage, and it was the largest of three artillery fortresses built at the time along this stretch of coast. Together with Sandown Castle, on the other side of Deal, which was largely demolished in the nineteenth century, and Walmer Castle (also in the care of English Heritage), Deal formed an important link in a chain of coastal defences that stretched from Hull to Milford Haven in Wales. While Walmer Castle has been extensively adapted, Deal still retains something of its Tudor appearance.

Deal has played an active role in history. Anne of Cleves visited Deal Castle on her way from Flanders to marry Henry VIII, and the castle underwent a bitter siege in 1648, during the Civil War. It was extensively modernised between 1729 and 1732 and although it was of diminishing military use, it retained a role as a fortress until the end of the Napoleonic wars.

This guidebook begins with a tour of the castle, including the gatehouse, the bastions and the keep, where there is an interactive exhibition on the castle. The tour is followed by a detailed history of the site, from Tudor times to the twentieth century.

❖ CONTENTS ❖

Published by English Heritage
1 Waterhouse Square, 138-142 Holborn, London EC1N 2ST
Copyright © English Heritage 1998
First published by English Heritage 1998
Reprinted 2000, 2003, 2005, 2008, 2011, 2012
Revised reprint 2014, Reprinted 2015
Visit our website at www.english-heritage.org.uk

Photographs by English Heritage Photographic Unit
and copyright of English Heritage, unless otherwise stated

Edited by Susannah Lawson
Designed by Derek Lee
Printed in England by Park Communications Ltd
C47, 06/15, 01971, ISBN 978 1 85074 697 3

TOUR OF THE CASTLE

INTRODUCTION

This tour starts, appropriately, at the gatehouse. It begins by looking at the main defences of the castle and examining the elaborate system for protecting the courtyard and keep, in case enemy soldiers stormed the main gate or succeeded in crossing the moat. Next, the tour moves to the keep, the heart of the castle, to look at the living quarters. The tour ends in the great basement storerooms with a visit to the exhibition and 'the Rounds', the complex and extraordinary defensible passage which winds around behind the inner face of the moat and which enabled the garrison to fire across the moat floor. The whole tour takes about an hour.
Go back out through the shop and gatehouse to the entrance, to get a better view of the castle from the outside. From the inside, it is not always easy to appreciate the enormous care which went into the castle's planning. But from the outside, Deal Castle shows

all the characteristic features which distinguish Henry VIII's chain of artillery fortresses of the late 1530s. Dominating the centre is the circular keep with its lantern (the present lantern dates from the early eighteenth century, but it is on the site of an original one). Attached to the keep are six semi-circular bastions or lunettes. These overlook a narrow courtyard and the six great bastions, which project from the outer curtain wall and which carried the main armament of heavy guns. North of the gatehouse bastion, part of the northern curtain wall still retains its original broad, rounded parapets. The crenellated battlements elsewhere (above the entrance, for example) form part of an extensive refurbishment of the castle undertaken between 1729 and 1732.

THE GATEHOUSE

The gatehouse is formed inside the western bastion. Its location on the

The Keep
This contained living quarters for the garrison and the captain. Food and ammunition would have been stored in the basement.

The Inner Bastions
These were designed to defend the courtyard and the rear of the main bastions.

'The Rounds'
A narrow passageway that runs round the inner face of the moat, allowing defenders to fire at attackers in the moat.

The Gatehouse
This was the main entrance to the castle, originally protected by a drawbridge.

The Courtyard
This was primarily a route for communication, but in a siege, it could serve as a kind of inner moat.

The Moat
This was never designed to hold water - its sheer scale, and the outer wall were sufficient protection.

The Outer Bastions
These were designed to mount the castle's heaviest guns. When first, constructed, they had guns at two levels.

Aerial view of the castle, showing the main stopping-points on the tour

landward side of the castle suggests that this was primarily a coastal fortress designed to prevent attack from the sea. It used to have an upper storey but this was removed in the eighteenth century. If you turn round and look across the road, you will see the remains of a substantial walled garden, once used by the governor or captain of the castle.

The moat surrounding the castle was never designed to hold water - its sheer scale and the vertical stone outer wall in themselves providing formidable obstacles. The approach to the gatehouse is across a stone causeway which leads to a modern bridge. Originally, Henry VIII's engineers would have built a draw-bridge here. How this worked is uncertain, but the two circular holes above the gate may have been for ropes used to haul up the bridge. The pulleys in the roof of the entrance passage relate to a later lifting bridge, perhaps installed during the Napoleonic wars in the early nineteenth century.

Above the entrance are the remains of a stone plaque. This was reduced in height, probably during alterations to the gatehouse in the early eighteenth century. An etching of the castle in 1649 by Hollar (below) shows its original size and suggests that it may well once have had a carving of the royal coat-of-arms, such as survives at the contemporary St Mawes Castle in Cornwall. Inside the entrance

View of the moat to the north of the entrance

Above the entrance are the remains of a stone plaque, and two holes which may once have been for ropes used to haul up the drawbridge

passage are the remains of the grooves for a portcullis, once operated from a now-vanished chamber above. In the roof of the passageway are five holes designed

Etching of Deal Castle, c.1649, by Hollar. This is the best illustration showing the castle much as originally constructed

The massive iron-studded doors to the castle

The holes above the entrance allowed defenders to drop missiles on attackers below

to allow defenders above to rain down missiles or to use hand-guns on any attackers below. The massive oak doors with their iron studs and wicket gate are almost certainly original and are among the best preserved for their date.

Inside the doors is the entrance hall. Clearly visible here are the three main materials used in the original construction of the castle. The Tudor bricks probably came from local sources, while the rough, grey-coloured Kentish ragstone came from quarries near Maidstone. The creamy-coloured Caen stone, which originated from quarries in Normandy, probably came from the destruction of a local monastery. This seems highly likely, as some of the stones are carved. (There is one carved piece just above the window

into the shop, and another to the right of the lamp on the opposite wall.)

The inner doors which lead to the courtyard are carefully offset from the outer ones to prevent attackers from charging straight through. This arrangement also meant that a gun could be positioned in the courtyard to fire through an embrasure aligned on the outer doors. Originally, the inner doors were deliberately arranged to open outwards into the courtyard. This was to prevent an attacker inside the gatehouse from barring these doors from within, and turning the gatehouse into an independent stronghold. In the north wall of the entrance hall is the remains of a gunport, while on the south side is the guardroom, or porter's lodge, overlooking the entrance hall (this is now the castle shop). Within this can be seen a south-facing gunport. *Go back through the shop and into the courtyard.*

THE OUTER BASTIONS AND THE COURTYARD

This squat, low-lying fortress was designed to house the maximum number of guns. Its walls were deliberately kept as low as possible to present the minimum target to the guns of a besieger. The great thickness of the walls also allowed them to withstand a considerable bombardment. There were two main types of weapons in the castle: the main armament of heavy guns used to attack a hostile fleet or army at a distance and much smaller hand-guns for fighting at closer quarters. The gun openings or embrasures in the castle clearly reflect these two distinct types of weapons.

When first constructed, the main, outer bastions were hollow, allowing each, with the exception of the gatehouse, to have guns at ground level and on the roofs. However, they were filled solid in the 1570s. In the eighteenth century their parapets were largely reformed, but parts of the original rounded Tudor parapets still remain on the north-west and south-west bastions which flank the gatehouse.

The outer bastions, including the gatehouse, were designed to mount the castle's heaviest guns. The narrow courtyard in which you are standing, which encircles the castle between the inner and outer bastions, was primarily a route for communication. In a close siege, it could also serve as a land of inner moat, for it is overlooked by gun embrasures in the keep, and defenders could also fire into it from the gorges or rear of the outer bastions. The only door to the keep itself lies, not where a visitor might expect, opposite the gatehouse, but eccentrically placed in the southern inner bastion. This simple arrangement ensured that an attacker who had forced the gatehouse still had to pass nearly half of these inner defences before reaching the entrance to the keep.

It is worth walking round the main bastions of the castle before going inside the keep, as there are fine views of the coast from here. *Go up the stairs on your right to the south-west bastion.* If you look out from this bastion, you can see the former buildings of Deal barracks. Many of these date from the late eighteenth century, a reflection of the continuing military importance and vulnerability of this stretch of coast. Although last used by the Royal Marines, they were predominantly army barracks; part of these buildings was also used as a naval hospital until the end of the Napoleonic wars in the early nineteenth century. *Walk round to the south-east bastion, facing the sea.*

On the seaward bastions are mounted four 32-pounder guns from around 1800. (The truck carriages are modern replicas.) These are known as Blomefield pattern guns

Blomefield pattern guns of c.1800 on the outer bastions, which were designed to mount the castle's heaviest guns

after improvements made by Major General Sir Thomas Blomefield, appointed in 1780 as Inspector of Ordnance and Superintendent of the Royal Brass Foundry at Woolwich. *Walk round to the next bastion, the eastern bastion.*

The red brick retaining wall to the rear of the eastern bastion is virtually all that remains of the extension to the captain's house, built over this part of the courtyard in 1730 and later enlarged again. A German bomb demolished most of it during the Second World War; after the war a decision was taken to reinstate this side of the keep to more of its original appearance. *Walk round to the northeast bastion; then go down the steps and back into the courtyard.* On your right are the remains of a shot furnace. This was used for heating cannon balls to a red heat. Although it was hazardous loading these into guns,

they could be very effective when fired into the wooden hulls of warships, as the Spanish had found to their cost in 1782 during the siege of Gibraltar. (During this famous siege, which lasted from 1779-83, the Spaniards and French tried unsuccessfully to capture the Rock from its British garrison. Repeated landward assaults failed, so the besiegers carefully converted ten old warships into floating gun batteries. On 13 September 1782 these were towed into position. Behind the British defences, the kilns for heating shot were readied. By the end of the night, every single floating battery was a blazing wreck, its crew suffering horrendous casualties. All over Europe, military engineers noted the success of the shot furnaces.) *Walk back past the gatehouse and shop and round the courtyard until you reach the entrance to the keep on your left.*

The remains of a shot furnace which was used for heating cannon balls

THE KEEP

Unlike a medieval castle, which was usually a permanent family home as well as a fortification, Deal was purely a garrison fortress. As such, its accommodation was more spartan. When completed, Deal had living quarters for a captain, thirty-four soldiers, a trumpeter and a drummer. They would all have been lodged within the keep and possibly the gatehouse. The basement of the keep would have been used for stores and ammunition, with most of the garrison accommodated on the ground floor. The first floor would largely have been the preserve of the captain and any distinguished visitors or fellow officers. Over the centuries, the exterior of the keep has been altered. Gun embrasures, for example, have been converted into windows to increase daylight within the building (the sash windows are all eighteenth- and nineteenth-century modifications of earlier openings). The interior of the keep has also been altered as its uses have changed. With the departure of a permanent garrison and the construction of the adjoining captain's house in the early 1730s, the keep itself seems to have taken on a more domestic role, mirroring similar changes at nearby Walmer Castle.

View of the inner bastions looking to the gatehouse

opening, but these have now all been converted into windows. This symmetrical arrangement extended all round the keep, ensuring that the courtyard could be swept by gunfire

The ground floor

Walk through the entrance to the keep, into the southern of the small, inner bastions. Note the fine rib-vaulted ceiling inside. There are four firing positions in this entrance passage, which were used to protect the doorway. Two remain unaltered. The height of the sills in these clearly indicates that they were intended for hand-weapons and not cannons. If you look through these openings you will see that they overlook or command the face of the next bastion. There was originally a series of larger gunports in between each

This opening on the ground floor of the keep allowed defenders to fire at attackers in the courtyard. The flue above allowed the smoke of the gunpowder to clear. (The window is an eighteenth-century modification of this Tudor embrasure)

The remains of the living quarters on the ground floor of the keep. There is a series of brick ovens built into the far wall, indicating the position of the original kitchen

and nobody could approach the keep without becoming a target for the defenders. The circular shaft to the rear of this entrance bastion, on your right, contains a staircase to the basement which is accessible from within the main body of the keep. *Walk through the doorway into the inner part of the keep.*

The main part of the ground floor of the keep is a circular space divided into a series of segmental-shaped rooms by walls radiating out from a small round tower in the centre. The round tower contains the main stairs to the first floor; within its foot is the castle well in the basement below. On the outer perimeter of the ground floor are the six semi-circular bastions with their gunports for defending the courtyard and covering the rear of the main bastions beyond. The doorways to the inner bastions give a good indication of the thickness of the main wall at this level.

The ground floor would have been used by the soldiers of the Tudor garrison, but we have no detailed

The remains of an original Tudor fireplace on the ground floor

❖ GARRISON LIFE ❖

During its active life, as a fortress, Deal Castle had between sixteen and eighteen gunners. They earned about 6d a day in the Tudor period and lived on the ground floor of the castle, where they would have shared rooms and had a fairly communal life. It is likely that a number were married and had their wives and children with them. Their main peacetime tasks were to guard the castle and look after its armament, and to practise occasionally with the heavy weapons and with the lighter hand-guns and bows and arrows. They would also have guarded any cargoes brought here from wrecked ships. Garrison life was not strictly regulated and it is known that the men supplemented their income by taking casual work in the town. In wartime, their numbers where increased by local recruits. In 1618 it is recorded that the garrisons of Deal and Sandown worshipped at the parish church of St Leonard as neither castles had chapels. The poor state of repair of the castles then meant that many of the garrison lived in Deal itself.

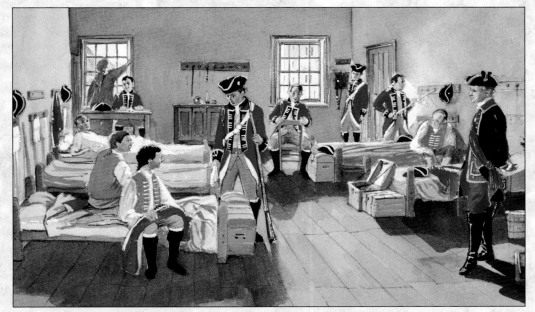

Reconstruction drawing of the Georgian barracks at Dover Castle by Terry Ball. Soldiers garrisoned at Deal would also have lived this kind of communal life. By this time they may even have been quartered in the new barracks nearby

evidence for the original layout here. The soldiers would have lived a communal life, eating and sleeping in one large room or hall, just as did their predecessors in the great halls of medieval castles. The main door probably led straight into this living space and other rooms would have been partitioned-off, using timber framing with wattle and daub infill panels.

The fireplace to the left of the entrance is part of the original work of around 1540, although it has been considerably altered. Its location is perhaps further evidence for the garrison hall being here. On the right-hand side of the room are a series of brick ovens built into the rear of the south-east, inner bastion. The larger

The sunken pit beneath this fireplace may once have been part of a forge, used for maintaining weapons for the garrison

of these is original, as is the great kitchen fireplace. The kitchen would have been separated from the rest of the ground floor by partitions which have long since gone. *Walk round the rooms on the ground floor in an anti-clockwise direction. Take time to explore the bastions as you go round.*

The rooms beyond the former kitchen give few clues to their sixteenth-century use. The room right next to the garrison hall may once have been sleeping quarters, perhaps for married soldiers of the garrison or for the sick. *Walk through into the next room.* The sunken pit under the fireplace in the northern wall suggests that there might once have been a workshop here. The pit itself may have been part of a hearth or forge - it is perhaps not too fanciful to suggest that this might have been the location for the garrison armourer's workshop. *Go through the door into the bastion to get a better view of the remains of the forge. Then retrace your steps and go through the next door into the chapel.*

This chapel was created after the First World War by Field Marshal Sir John French, first earl of Ypres, soon after his appointment in 1923 as captain of Deal Castle. The chapel was restored and re-hallowed by the bishop of Dover in 1980. There is no evidence for a chapel in the castle in the sixteenth century. *Walk through the door at the other end of the chapel, and back into the garrison hall. Stop by the stairs on the left.*

When it was first built, the central staircase was an outstanding example of the skills of Tudor carpenters and joiners. It was originally a double staircase, with each circular stair starting off at ground level from the two existing doorways opposite each other and using the same central newel post. Clear evidence for this arrangement is preserved in the mortice slots in the oak newel post which show the position of the second set of stairs which led up to the roof. The present staircase to the first floor is a reconstruction of some fifty years ago when a later staircase was being removed. Five of the Tudor timber steps were found embedded in this later staircase and have been incorporated in the reconstruction. They are

The interior of the lantern on the first floor of the keep; this lit the central stairs

readily identifiable from the underneath by their rough-hewn surfaces. *Go up the stairs to the first floor and through the first door on the right.* In these rooms is a series of portraits of some of the captains of Deal Castle.

The first floor

The first floor owes much of its present appearance to the extensive modernisation begun in the late 1720s, almost certainly during the captaincy of Admiral Sir John Norris. By that date, the castle's role as a fortress was declining and the captain was as much concerned with his domestic comforts as with the needs of defence. The handsome timber panelling was installed, in some cases replacing or covering Tudor wattle and daub plaster partitions. The

The exterior of the lantern on the top of the keep

panelling of the outer stone wall, the masking of the Tudor fireplaces and their replacement by eighteenth-century grates, was all part of this attempt to improve what would by then have been seen as an old-fashioned castle, lacking in dignity. (It is now possible to see some of the Tudor fireplaces, discovered behind the outer panelling some fifty years ago.) Not all the Tudor internal partitions were swept away at that time. At the western end of the landing, just behind the top of the stairs, an oak doorway leads to a small suite of Tudor rooms which still have some of their plank partitions. These rooms are not open to visitors, but a Tudor garderobe or latrine can be seen in the thickness of the outer wall just to the south of them, accessible from the room at the far end of this suite of rooms. *Go back out into the main corridor.*

This corridor once led to a set of rooms built onto the Tudor castle in the eighteenth century. They were destroyed by enemy action in the

---

❖ THE CAPTAINS OF DEAL CASTLE ❖

The captain of the castle was the senior military officer in charge of the garrison. The captains of the three castles of Deal, Walmer and Sandown in turn took their orders from the Lord Warden of the Cinque Ports whose official residence until 1708 was at Dover Castle. Many of the early captains of Deal were local men – the first, Thomas Wingfield, was a citizen of Sandwich who was appointed as one of the officials in charge of the construction of the castle in 1539. One of the longest serving was Captain William

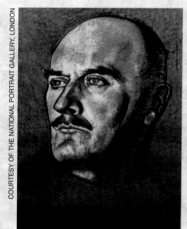

Portrait of Field Marshall Allenby, before 1926, by Eric Henri Kennington. Allenby was captain of Deal from 1925 to 1926

COURTESY OF THE NATIONAL PORTRAIT GALLERY, LONDON

Byng. He held office from 1608 until the castle passed into Parliamentary control at the outbreak of The Civil War in 1642. He was briefly re-appointed in 1660. During peacetime, captains could be kept busy acting as agents for the Lord Warden in claiming ownership of any wrecks in the vicinity. As the castle's military importance declined from the end of the seventeenth century, the post of captain of Deal Castle was increasingly seen as an honorary one, a reward for distinguished service to the Crown.

Graffiti on the outside of the lantern on top of the keep produced by soldiers stationed at Deal in the early eighteenth century. These graffiti probably represent the huts or tents of army regiments temporarily based near the castle

Second World War, but from the 1730s they formed the principal rooms of the captain's house. We have no precise knowledge of how any of the rooms within the Tudor castle were used, but it is reasonable to assume that up to the eighteenth century this first floor was used by the captain of the castle as his private accommodation. With the construction of the new lodgings to the east, these rooms probably all became bedrooms.

Go through the first door on your left, into the Battery Office (a name referring to its use in the Second World War). In this room a small area of the original sixteenth- century wattle and daub partitioning has been revealed beneath later panelling. *When you have finished in these rooms, go back down the stairs to the ground floor.*

Go through the doorway on the other side of the garrison hall and down the stairs to the basement.

The basement

At the foot of the stairs on your left is a broad passage linking the basement with a postern gate which gives access to the floor of the moat. Just beside this postern gate a narrow passageway runs right round the outer bastions, known as 'the Rounds'. From this passage no less than fifty-three gunports overlook the moat, allowing defenders to fire hand-guns or arrows at attackers. The passageway has a series of right-angled turns which are overlooked by internal loops to allow the garrison to defend itself if an enemy force succeeded in gaining entry through one of the postern gates.

The basement of the keep, which was used for storing food, fuel and ammunition

Although it is unlikely that there would have been sufficient men or weapons for all these firing positions, the Tudor designers were thorough in their work. At regular intervals in the passageway there are small brick recesses for lighting and for storing ammunition, while in the ceiling above are a series of smoke-vents - absolutely essential if the defenders were not to be choked by the dense smoke produced by gunpowder.

It is possible to walk a complete circle of 'the Rounds', but most visitors will probably choose to see half and to return to the main basement by means of the northern passageway, as they are dark and sometimes get flooded.

The basement has a fine rib-vaulted ceiling which curves round the central pillar containing the castle well. The main space is divided into three rooms by substantial cross-walls. The variety of materials, including cobbles, used in the construction of this part of the castle, is perhaps indicative of the speed of building and the need to use whatever materials were to hand. The basement was the principal storage area of the castle where food, fuel and ammunition would have been stockpiled to supply the garrison during a siege. For safety's sake here at Deal, the gun-powder was probably stored in one of the separate chambers which open off the basement and lie under the

❖ FOOD FOR THE GARRISON ❖

When the Royalist garrison of 224 surrendered to Parliamentary forces on 25 August 1648, the following items of food and ammunition were found within the castle.

5 barrels of gunpowder
10 hogsheads and a half of wheat
10 Holland cheeses
10 Suffolk cheeses
12 firkins of butter
2 hogsheads of beef
20 pieces of pork in salt
100 pieces of pork in water
17 Norsea Codd in water
8 pieces of beef in water
2 pieces of pork ready to dresse
1 barrel of pease
100 loaves of bread baked, beside Beare etc.

This list shows the sort of food and drink which sustained the soldiers when fresh produce was unobtainable. This basic diet, used both for garrison troops and sailors, altered little from the medieval period until the invention of canning and refrigeration in the nineteenth century. Until then, almost the only preservative available was salt and most foods had to be packed in barrels.

keep bastions. One of these, on the north-eastern side, still has its copper-sheathed door, a protective material which clearly indicates that it was once used as a gunpowder store. This may date from the eighteenth century when copper sheathing was added to reduce the risk of sparks, but there is no reason to suppose that the space was not used for gunpowder before then.

This wooden mangle, used for pressing clothes, dates from the nineteenth century, when this room was probably used as a laundry

Go through the door into the next room (the tour goes anti-clockwise round the basement). In this room, there is a large wooden mangle from the nineteenth century, used for pressing clothes. It is possible that this room was once used as a laundry.

Go out of this room into the passage and turn left to the well in the centre of the basement. This was used to supply the castle with water. *After you have seen the well, go back up the stairs to the main courtyard.*

HISTORY OF THE CASTLE

THE CONSTRUCTION OF THE CASTLE

Deal, Walmer and the now largely destroyed Sandown Castle were known as the three 'castles in the Downs'. They were built at great speed between 1539 and 1540 by Henry VIII to form an important link in a chain of coastal defences that stretched from Hull to Milford Haven in Wales. They were designed by the king to protect himself against a feared invasion by the Catholic powers of Europe, and they represented the first systematic attempt to protect likely landing places since the Roman forts of the Saxon Shore over 1200 years earlier.

Henry VIII's break with the Roman Catholic church in the early 1530s, the annulment of his

A painting of the three 'castles in the Downs', as they appeared in the early eighteenth century

Portrait of Henry VIII, c. 1536, by an unknown artist. Henry was responsible for the construction of Deal

COURTESY OF THE NATIONAL PORTRAIT GALLERY, LONDON

marriage to Catherine of Aragon, aunt of the Emperor Charles V, and then the destruction of the English monasteries, had all worsened relations with continental states. But as long as the two principal Catholic military powers on the Continent were openly hostile to each other, war with England was unlikely. Then in June 1538 Francis I of France and Charles V signed a peace treaty at almost exactly the same time as a papal Bull was published excommunicating Henry VIII. An invasion of England under the banner of a Catholic crusade suddenly became a distinct possibility. Fortunately for Henry VIII, the time taken to raise forces and obtain ships, together with the need to avoid a winter crossing of the Channel, meant that an attack before the spring of 1539 was unlikely.

Early in 1539, Henry VIII and his officials began their preparations in earnest. Ships of the Royal Navy were brought into commission and manned, able-bodied men were recruited and weapons and mercenaries were sought in Hamburg and Antwerp. A chain of warning beacons was readied around the coast. In themselves, these mobilisations might not have been decisive against a well-equipped invasion force able to evade or defeat the king's fleet. However, a crucial element of these preparations, and the one which has provided a lasting memorial to these turbulent times, was the construction

of the great chain of coastal forts. In February 1539, the king ordered commissioners to survey the southern coasts of England - the part of the country most at risk from an invasion from France or the Low Countries – and to chose locations for defence works to protect likely invasion beaches, fleet anchorages, harbours and ports and the new dockyard at Portsmouth. Henry VIII's prime aim was to prevent an enemy force actually landing. An invasion force is at its most defenceless as it struggles ashore, so the king's new castles were carefully sited not only to be able to fire on hostile ships but also to command any adjacent landing places.

The coast at Deal was considered to be especially vulnerable. This part of Kent is near to mainland Europe, while its long shingle beach close to deep water allows easy landing. To the north lie the inhospitable Sandwich Flats and to the south are the sheer cliffs of Dover. Dover harbour itself was too small and was reasonably defended. Moreover, an invader here had to subdue Dover Castle. Although largely obsolete by then, its sheer scale would have made this a formidable undertaking.

Deal had one further significant advantage. Some six miles offshore lie the Goodwin Sands. Greatly feared by mariners in fog and storms, the sands extend roughly parallel to the coast for some ten miles and vary in width between two and three miles. At low tide, the sands are exposed and over the centuries have proved to be a graveyard for hundreds of ships and sailors. But the Downs, the stretch of water between these and the coast, provides a relatively safe anchorage for shipping in most winds. Even today, a considerable number of vessels can be seen sheltering here during stormy weather. For this reason too, the Downs long remained a principal rendezvous for the Royal Navy, and Deal traders made a good living supplying food and provisions both to the fleet and to merchant shipping from all over northern Europe. The area was also a convenient landing point and a place of embarkation, a role it fulfilled well into the nineteenth century. In 1495 Perkin Warbeck (a pretender to the throne) had chosen to land his forces at Deal. The same beach and sheltered anchorage could be powerful attractions to another

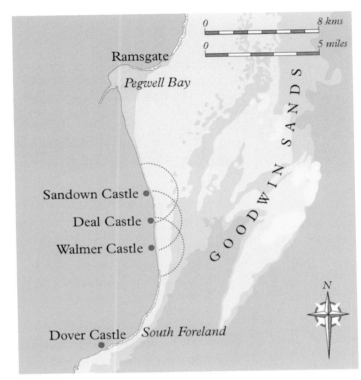

Map of the Downs and the Kent coast, showing the positions of Sandown, Deal and Walmer with their ranges of fire and also Dover Castle

DEAL MARITIME AND LOCAL HISTORY MUSEUM

The Goodwin Sands have proved to be a graveyard for hundreds of ships and sailors. This late nineteenth-century engraving by C. Butterworth shows the south Goodwin lightship firing a distress rocket in response to a shipwreck

A mid-nineteenth-century photograph of Sundown Castle, which was largely demolished in the 1860s

Walmer Castle from the gardens; unlike Deal, which has retained more of its fort-like appearance, Walmer has been transformed over the years into a country house, official residence of the Lords Warden of the Cinque Ports

invading army less than half a century later.

Today, Deal and Walmer form one continuous conurbation, but until well into the nineteenth century they remained distinct communities separated by low-lying farmland. Henry VIII himself knew the area and in February 1539, 'a device by the king' proposed the construction of three bulwarks or forts to protect the Downs. The commissioners put in charge of the defences of this area

were both local men – Sir Edward Ryngeley and Thomas Wingfield – and they may well have been instrumental in adding a further four earth bulwarks and a defensible trench or covered way which linked all seven fortifications over a distance of two and a half miles. The trench itself did not survive for long, but the four earth bulwarks were still standing in the eighteenth century, although long abandoned. Together, these fortifications were formidable and ideally placed to protect the nearby shipping and the beach.

The three principal stone fortresses were Sandown, Deal and Walmer. Sandown was largely demolished in the middle of the nineteenth century, while Walmer has been the official residence of the Lords Warden of the Cinque Ports since 1708, and has been modified for this more peaceful role. Deal, the largest of the three 'castles in the Downs' has been least altered and retains more of its fort-like appearance.

Construction was underway on all these defences by April 1539. Such was the urgency engendered by a very real threat of invasion that by May 1400 were at work with more men being drafted in. A strike in June by labourers demanding pay of 6d a day was ended by Ryngeley who had nine of the ringleaders gaoled. Although we have no precise details of the progress of work, it would seem probable that the skilled craftsmen

❖ ANNE OF CLEVES ❖

Anne of Cleves was briefly the fourth of Henry VIII's six wives. The king's ministers were anxious to secure Protestant allies on the Continent, which is why they sought this marriage in 1539. Henry VIII had to rely on the reports of his ambassadors to the Duke of Cleves for his information on Anne's beauty and charms, as well as on a portrait by Holbein. Just after Christmas 1539, Anne and her retinue landed at Deal. She was briefly entertained at the castle, which was not yet

Engraving of Anne of Cleves, after Holbein Anne visited Deal on her way to marry Henry VIII

COURTESY OF THE NATIONAL PORTRAIT GALLERY, LONDON

complete, before moving on to Dover Castle for a few days; she then set out for the king's palace at Greenwich. Impatient to meet her, Henry travelled to Rochester in disguise. The king was bitterly disappointed. 'I am ashamed that men have so praised her as they have done, and I like her not.' Nevertheless, the ceremony went ahead, although Henry never consummated the marriage. The following July he divorced her; She lived on for a further eighteen years in England.

---

and the bulk of the labour force would have concentrated on the three masonry castles. We know that Deal Castle was sufficiently complete to allow Anne of Cleves to dine in some state there after she had disembarked nearby in December 1539, on her way to become Henry VIII's fourth wife.

Labourers and unskilled workmen set to work on the construction of the intermediate earth bulwarks and the linking defensible ditch. By the summer of 1540 it would appear, from surviving accounts, that money was then being concentrated on the

ditch, with final payments for all the works taking place on 11 September 1540.

The loss of the Tudor building accounts for these castles means that we know far less about the initial construction of the 'castles in the Downs' than we do about contemporary fortresses such as Camber in East Sussex. There is evidence that lead from the monastic houses then being demolished, because of the Dissolution of the Monasteries, was used for roofing, and it seems highly probable that some of the stone and possibly the timber came from the same

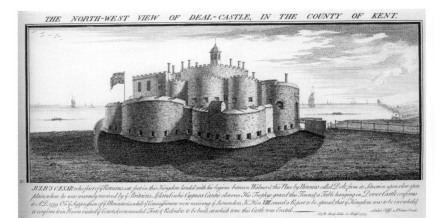

THE NORTH-WEST VIEW OF DEAL-CASTLE, IN THE COUNTY OF KENT.

Engraving of Deal Castle, 1735, by the Buck Brothers. This shows it after modernisation in the early 1730s (Compare with the Hollar engraving on p.5)

sources. Certainly all three of these castles have re-used stone visible in their walls, and its availability would have done much to speed construction. Where new stone was needed, Kentish Rag was supplied from limestone quarries near Maidstone.

Although Henry VIII took a very close personal interest in the design of the fortifications, and is known to have made a 'device' or plan for the defence works of the Downs, the actual construction work was the responsibility of the two local commissioners. They were helped by experienced staff, master masons and master carpenters, who had been working on the great royal palaces at Hampton Court and Nonsuch. These men translated the king's wishes into the final designs and ensured that all these royal fortifications of the late 1530s and early 1540s conform to a common style.

The designer responsible for the three castles is not known. The only military engineer known by name at the Downs was Stephen von Haschenperg, who is known to have worked at Camber and Sandgate Castles, and who apparently had responsibility for the four earth bulwarks. He came from Moravia in what is now the Czech Republic, but beyond that, little is known about him and it is unlikely that he had any input into Deal Castle.

THE ORIGINAL DESIGN OF DEAL CASTLE

Deal Castle was the largest of the three 'castles in the Downs', and its design was very different from the traditional medieval castle. These castles generally had high outer walls, to protect the garrison and buildings inside and to give the archers of the garrison additional range. Such walls, however, were found to be highly vulnerable after the development of heavy guns and the introduction of artillery siege trains by military leaders in the latter part of the fifteenth century. Military engineers were therefore forced to devise new styles of fortification which did not have high, thin walls, but instead had thick, squat walls to present less of a target. Generally, the walls were considerably thicker than their medieval predecessors and they were frequently backed by wide earth ramparts, which provided space to mount defensive artillery, as well as helping strengthen the masonry to withstand the shock of bombardment.

With their semi-circular bastions arranged symmetrically round central, circular towers, Henry VIII's castles were logical developments from the circular gun towers then

❖ TUDOR WEAPONS ❖

Deal Castle owes its design to the introduction of effective guns and gunpowder at the very end of the fifteenth century. Henry VIII took a keen interest in these weapons, encouraging their design and production. This new heavy ordnance, cast from both brass and iron, came in numerous sizes and had a bewildering variety of names – cannon, demi-cannon, culverins, sacres minions and falcons, to name a few. All fired solid shot of varying sizes, either stone or cast-iron with effective ranges of up to perhaps 1,000 metres. Hand-guns were also coming into use, but they were cumbersome and had a slow rate of fire compared to bows. Deal Castle was designed specifically to mount heavy ordnance, but many of the old hand-weapons remained as part of the garrison equipment. A 1518 inventory of weapons mentions a number of heavy iron and brass guns, along with hand-guns ('arquebusses'), but it also lists pikes and bows and arrows, the standard equipment of medieval warfare.

THE MARY ROSE TRUST PORTSMOUTH

Cast bronze nuzzle-loading Bastard Culverin, on reproduction gun carriage, recovered from the Mary Rose

This 1539 drawing of an artillery fort shows a castle which looks similar in design to Deal, with guns mounted on outer and inner bastions filled with sand to give extra protection to the gunners

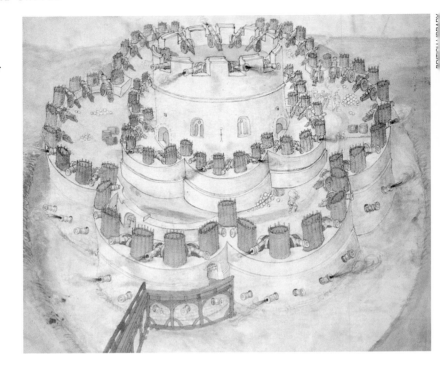

used in England and northern France to protect harbour entrances from hostile shipping. These gun towers, not dissimilar to the later Martello Towers such as Dymchurch, started to be constructed in coastal areas of northern Europe in the late fifteenth century. One at Camber in East Sussex, built in 1513, was later to form the core of one of Henry VIII's more powerful fortresses.

The heart of Deal Castle is the central tower, strongly constructed to carry guns on its roof. Around its

This 1539 illustration of an artillery fort shows a simpler version of the Deal design which omits the small inner bastions

base are a cluster of six small semi-circular bastions or lunettes overlooking the outer curtain wall. This has a further six massive rounded bastions, one of which forms the gatehouse. These outer bastions were originally hollow, allowing four guns on their flat roofs to fire through parapet openings or embrasures, and three to fire through gunports in chambers below. The gatehouse had one fewer gunport. In between each bastion there was a single embrasure in the curtain wall. This powerful design enabled Henry's engineers to mount no fewer than sixty-six guns in four tiers. For defence at closer quarters, a narrow gallery runs round at basement level, its firing-loops permitting the defenders to cover the moat with up to fifty-three hand-guns. In all, there were at least 145 openings for weapons of one sort or another. However, there is no evidence that the castle was ever armed to this extent, while later alterations have obscured or destroyed some of these original arrangements.

THE TUDOR CASTLE

When Anne of Cleves landed at Deal on 27 December 1539, she stayed briefly at the castle, then described as 'newly built'. This was probably an optimistic statement as it was not until the following autumn that it was sufficiently complete for Thomas Wingfield to be appointed as first captain of the castle. He was given thirty-four soldiers, a trumpeter and a drummer, as well as a strict set of rules for regulating garrison life. Like his fellow captains at Walmer and Sandown, he took his orders from the Lord Warden of the Cinque Ports at Dover Castle. (Dover was the official residence of the Lords Warden until 1708, when the duke of Dorset moved to Walmer.)

The invasion scare which had prompted the construction of Deal Castle had subsided even before the fortress was complete. However, along with Walmer and Sandown, its strategic importance was to ensure that Deal had a long life as a garrisoned fortress, a largely unbroken succession of captains remaining resident there into the nineteenth century. An inventory of the castle, made soon after the death of Henry VIII in 1547, lists an impressive

Aerial view of Dymchurch Martello Tower in Kent. The design of these early nineteenth-century defences was based on the simple gun towers which had been built on European coasts since the fifteenth century

*Reconstruction drawing by
Alan Sorrell of Deal Castle,
as newly completed in 1540*

variety of brass and iron guns and ammunition here, but it also includes 77 bows and 468 sheaves of arrows. A similar variety of weapons was found on board Henry VIII's warship, the Mary Rose, which sank off Spithead in 1545 and shows clearly the transitional nature of early Tudor weaponry.

Around 1570, the castle underwent a major alteration when all the main bastions, except for the gatehouse, were filled solid with earth. This might have been done to allow heavier guns to be mounted at parapet level, or it might have been an economy measure, perhaps prompted by the poor condition of the existing timber and lead roofs which served as gun platforms. Whatever the reason, by the Armada year of 1588, the castle mounted some sixteen guns of varying weights and calibre and the garrison was made up of one master gunner and sixteen gunners, a considerable reduction on the 1540 complement, and a number woefully inadequate to man all the guns simultaneously. No doubt that summer, these men joined in the frantic preparations as England sought to withstand another and far more serious Catholic crusade. News of the progress of the Armada up the Channel and of its skirmishes with Drake, Hawkins and Howard's ships would have been keenly followed. Seymour's small squadron, blockading Parma's forces in Dunkirk, was probably frequently seen off Deal, but the main battle passed the castle by. However, it is likely that the garrison witnessed from the castle ramparts the glow in the night sky as Howard sent his eight fire-ships in amongst the

❖ THE SPANISH ARMADA, 1588 ❖

The Armada was a huge fleet of around 130 ships, intended by Philip II of Spain to carry his invasion troops to England to end Elizabeth I's support for the Protestant Dutch rebels in the Spanish Netherlands. In July 1588, the Armada sailed from Corunna to embark the Spanish army in the Netherlands, then cross the Channel to England. In one of the most famous and prolonged battles fought by the Royal Navy, the English fleet under Howard, Drake and Hawkins harried the great Spanish galleons up the Channel. Off Calais, English fireships caused the Armada to break formation, and the ensuing fighting and storms destroyed more than half the Spanish fleet. Protestants throughout Europe hailed the victory as a divine judgement, while Elizabeth I caused a commemorative medal to be struck with the words, *'Afflavit Deus et dissipati sunt'*, ('God blew and they were scattered').

Spanish fleet off Calais in early August, and it may well have heard, against the rising wind, the sounds of the last battle off Gravelines in the Low Countries the following day. Although we have no direct evidence, it is likely that all the castles here remained fully manned and alert during the war years at the end of Elizabeth I's reign.

SEVENTEENTH CENTURY, CIVIL WAR AND SIEGE

In 1608 William Byng was appointed captain, a post he held until 1642. For much of his time, his main concern was to obtain money from the king to repair the castle. In 1616 the outer moat wall was breached in a storm. Further damage was caused to all three castles in 1622 when the captains petitioned the Lord Treasurer for help, saying that all were in increasing states of disrepair. Not surprisingly, garrison morale was low, with most men living in the town. French and Dutch ships using the Downs displayed increasing insolence, many refusing to dip their national flags to the

View of the castle from the beach. The crenellations date from the 1730s modernisation

castles as custom dictated. Worse still, the anchorage became a place of strife in the 1620s and 1630s as Dutch, French and Spanish ships and 'Dunkirkers' skirmished with each other, largely ignoring the English law forbidding foreign ships to engage in any act of war here. This culminated in a fierce battle in 1639 when a Spanish fleet, numbering some 140 warships and merchant ships, was driven into the Downs by the Dutch admiral, Martin van Tromp, intent on preventing the Spanish from landing reinforcements in the Low Countries. Despite considerable diplomatic activity in the ensuing month, a fierce fight broke out on 11 October. By the end of a day which had seen a small British fleet having to intervene to try to stop the fighting, twenty-four Spanish ships and two Dutch ships had run ashore between Deal and Walmer Castles, and Dover and Deal were filled with around 2,000 wounded and destitute Spanish sailors and troops. Perhaps surprisingly, there was very little damage in Deal from all the gunfire.

On the outbreak of the Civil War in 1642, the navy and the three castles (Deal, Walmer and Sandown) came into Parliamentary control. Some £600 was spent repairing Deal Castle and each of the three was given a further ten gunners to augment its garrison. It was not until 1648,

❖ THE KENTISH UPRISING OF 1648 ❖

The lengthy negotiations between Charles I, Parliament and the Parliamentary army after the king had surrendered at the end of the Civil War in 1646, led to increasing unrest in the country, culminating in 1648 in revolts in south Wales, Essex and Kent. Unrest had begun in Canterbury the previous December when the Presbyterian-led Parliament decreed, that Christmas should not be celebrated. The following May, leaders of the Canterbury riots were tried by a Parliamentary commission, but the jury refused to find the men guilty. Instead, a petition was circulated in the county asking that peace negotiations be concluded with the king, the Parliamentary army be disbanded and the rule of law be firmly re-established. When Parliament treated this as a rebellion, The Kentish petitioners resolved to fight. In late May 1648, naval ships anchored in the Downs sided with the rebels who also took over Deal, Walmer and Sandown. The main body of Kentish rebels was decisively defeated by Fairfax and the Parliamentary army in the bloody battle of Maidstone on 1 June.

however, that the castles saw action. That spring, tired of Parliamentary rule, large numbers of men in Kent took up arms on behalf of the king. The main insurrection, known as the Kentish uprising, was bloodily suppressed by Fairfax and the New Model Army at Maidstone on 1 June. But on the coast, naval vessels in the Downs had also declared for the king. Backed by this small fleet, Royalist forces had taken control of Sandown, Deal and Walmer and were laying siege to Dover Castle.

After defeating the rebels in Maidstone, Fairfax sent Colonel Rich with a party of soldiers to raise the siege of Dover. This was accomplished without difficulty on 5 June and his forces then turned their attention to the three 'castles in the Downs'. These, though, presented a more formidable challenge as they were being supplied by sea and, initially at any rate, Rich had very limited artillery. He first laid siege to Walmer, probably around 15 June, but it was 12 July before the castle was taken.

From Walmer the Parliamentary forces moved to Deal. This was to be an altogether more protracted and bloody affair. Here, Rich's initial lack of siege artillery and the inability of his small force to surround both Deal and Sandown Castles, placed him at a considerable disadvantage as the garrisons of the castles were able to come to each other's aid.

On 15 July a fleet of Royalist warships arrived under the command of James, Duke of York. An attempted landing was repulsed, but the fleet bombarded Parliamentary positions around Deal Castle. The following day, thirty Flemish ships arrived with some 1500 mercenaries. However, the arrival of this foreign army on Kentish soil in some ways was to prove counterproductive. Its presence incensed many people, enabling the Parliamentarian Sir Michael Livesey to raise forces within the county to come to Colonel Rich's aid. It also impressed on Parliament the seriousness of the situation and the need to send heavy artillery to Deal. The Royalist fleet lay off Deal for about a week before a probable lack of funds to pay the mercenaries forced its return to Holland. The Parliamentary forces in the meantime strengthened their siege works and trenches on the landward side of the castle.

On 28 July, the Royalist warships returned, this time under the command of the Prince of Wales, the future Charles II. In the course of the next three weeks there was a series of abortive Royalist attempts to land and relieve the garrison of Deal, which by now was coming under sustained fire from Parliamentary siege guns. The most ambitious attempt was made on the night of 13 August when 800 soldiers and sailors landed under cover of darkness. They marched inland before turning to attack the Parliamentary siege works and camp from the rear. Surprise might have been complete had not a deserter raised the alarm. In the ensuing fighting, the Royalists were heavily defeated and many were killed; 300 fled to Sandown Castle and less than 100 got safely back to the fleet.

On 18 August there was a further Royalist attempt to raise the siege, but this also failed. The day before, Oliver Cromwell had decisively defeated the Scottish forces at Preston in Lancashire, effectively ending all Royalist hopes of victory. A piece of paper giving news of this defeat was tied to an arrow and shot into Deal Castle on 23 August. Two days later, the garrison surrendered. On 5 September, the garrison at Sandown also laid down their arms and with the fall of this castle, the Kentish rebellion was at an end

After the Siege

After its capture, Colonel Rich was appointed captain of the castle, a post he was to retain to 1653. He reported the castle 'much torn' by the siege and needing at least £500 spent on repairs. Deal, Sandown and Walmer all had their damage made good and all were given Parliamentary garrisons.

The opening shots of the First Dutch War (1652–4) took place off Deal between British and Dutch warships. Although the castle was not directly involved, and although later naval actions in these wars took place elsewhere, the need to ensure that the castles could protect the anchorage had never been greater.

After the Restoration of Charles II in 1660, the garrison at Deal was maintained, but reduced by one in number to eighteen soldiers, or gunners, a porter, a lieutenant and a captain. These numbers were increased during the Second and Third Dutch Wars (1665–7 and 1672–4) when Deal, along with its neighbouring castles, helped guard the ships of the Royal Navy using the Downs anchorage. Although Dutch fleets sailed close to Deal during both wars, none of the castles saw any action.

The Castle Modernised

By the beginning of the eighteenth century, Deal Castle was seen as increasingly old-fashioned and of diminishing military use. The conversion of Walmer Castle in 1708 into the official residence of the Lord Warden of the Cinque Ports was a tacit admission that the days of these Tudor castles as major fortresses were largely over. Nevertheless, Deal Castle continued to mount guns – 11 culverins (cannons firing a shot of some eighteen pounds) were recorded there in 1728, and a captain

Engraving of Admiral Sir John Norris, captain of Deal Castle, 1741, by T. Burford. Norris was responsible for many of the 1730s alterations to the castle

continued to be appointed, although the post was by now probably chiefly valued for its title and the official accommodation. The town of Deal, meanwhile, was developing other military links. In the seventeenth century a small navy yard had been established to supply Royal Navy warships in the Downs; this remained in use until closure in 1864. The Time Ball Tower on the sea front, its ball falling down its mast to mark one o'clock to ships offshore, marks the location of the original naval yard, as well as indicating the importance of the anchorage here. In 1714, the Master-General of Ordnance, in charge of all the heavy weapons used by the army and navy, established land and sea ranges at Deal for gunnery practice. This led to the establishment of a military presence

in the town which remained unbroken until 1996; the principal monument today is the large complex of historic barracks to the west of the castle.

In the late 1720s, Deal Castle underwent extensive alterations to provide more comfortable accommodation. This parallels contemporary works at Walmer, suggesting a degree of rivalry between the captain, Admiral Sir John Norris and the Lord Warden, Lionel Cranfield, first duke of Dorset. In 1729 modest alterations were begun in Deal keep, then known as the king's lodgings, to provide a new powder magazine. This project rapidly grew in scope. A new house for the captain was built out from the keep on the seaward side and it was completed by 1732. The keep and the keep bastions had their parapets and battlements entirely rebuilt – a contractor was paid £52 9s 3d for carrying away 1399 loads of 'the rubbish of the old parapets' and throwing them into the sea. Inside the keep, the accommodation was extensively modernised and linked to the new lodgings by cutting through the outer wall on the eastern side. Some of the existing wainscotting was salvaged and reused in the new captain's lodgings, but much of the keep was provided with new panelling which still survives, especially on the first floor. The porter's lodge in the gatehouse was also modernised and given new fireplaces and chimneys, and in 1732 the finishing touch was provided by the purchase and installation on the rampart of a new sixty-foot high flagstaff. These alterations to the Tudor castle gave it much of the appearance it has retained to the present. The captain's house, however, was further extended and altered early in the nineteenth century. It was destroyed by a German bomber in the Second World War, allowing this part of the castle to be restored to its pre-1728 appearance during post-war repair work.

Later History

These eighteenth-century alterations effectively turned the castle into a marine residence, and the substitution of the more theatrical medieval-style crenellations for the rounded Tudor parapets was an outward sign that this was now principally a home. It nevertheless remained a fortress with its massive outer walls and solid bastions. During the Napoleonic wars at the end of the eighteenth century the castle was re-armed with nine 36-pounder guns, but here, as elsewhere along this vulnerable coast, temporary gun batteries or field works were constructed along the beach to deter invasion. Here, the guns of the castle also gave a measure of protection to the huge number of merchant ships, at times numbering more than 200, which regularly gathered in the Downs to await naval escorts to protect them against French warships

Engraving of Deal Castle, 1823, by William Daniell, showing the captain's house built on to the seaward side of the castle. This was destroyed in the Second World War

and privateers. In 1802, William Pitt, in his capacity as Prime Minister and Lord Warden of the Cinque Ports, appointed his friend and fellow MP Lord Carrington as captain of Deal Castle. Carrington played a notable local role, becoming lieutenant colonel of the second battalion of the Cinque Ports Volunteers, one of many such battalions raised during this war. He remained as captain until his death in 1838 and was the last captain to make substantial alterations to his official residence.

The end of the Napoleonic wars in 1815 marked the final use of the castle as a defence work. It remains an official residence for the captain of Deal, but in 1904 the War Department gave it to the Office of Works to restore and to open to visitors when it was not occupied. Perhaps the most famous of all the captains of the castle, and certainly the highest ranking, were the two field marshals who held the captaincy in succession between 1923 and 1926. Sir John French, first earl of Ypres, had an extraordinarily varied military career, which included taking part in Wolseley's expedition for the relief of General Gordon at Khartoum, serving with distinction in the Boer War and commanding the British expeditionary force to France in 1914. On being appointed captain of the castle in 1923, he made it his home and died here in 1925. He was succeeded by Field Marshal Allenby, whose career throughout the empire in some ways parallels that of his predecessor; he achieved his greatest fame for his capture of Jerusalem and Damascus from the Turks in the latter stages of the First World War. The castle ceased to be lived in regularly by the captain at the turn of the Second World War. It is now cared for by English Heritage.

Portrait of Sir John French, first earl of Ypres, by John Singer Sargent. French was captain of Deal from 1923 to 1925

BIBLIOGRAPHY

H. M. Colvin, *The History of the Kings' Works*, Vol. IV, part II, London, 1982

J. Laker, *History of Deal*, Deal, 1917

R. and B. Larn, *Shipwrecks of the Goodwin Sands*, Ashford, 1995

B. St. J. O'Neill, *Deal Castle*, 1966

Primary sources

The National Archives, WO 50/778

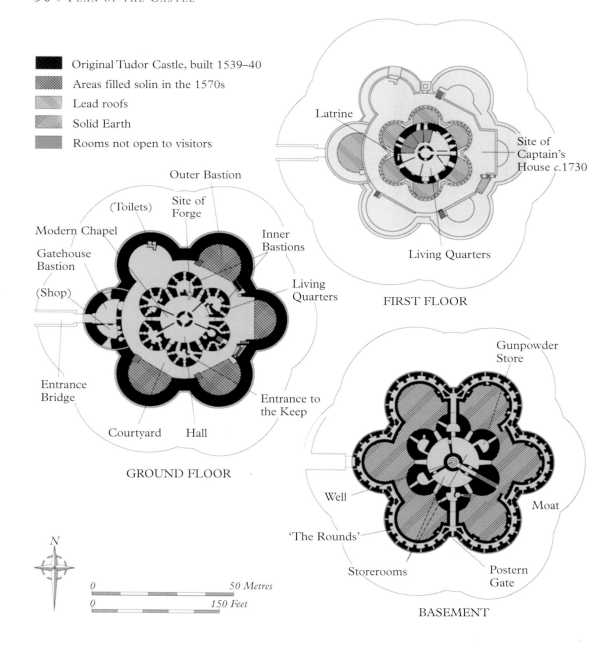

Original Tudor Castle, built 1539–40

Areas filled solin in the 1570s

Lead roofs

Solid Earth

Rooms not open to visitors

FIRST FLOOR

Latrine

Site of Captain's House c.1730

Living Quarters

Outer Bastion

(Toilets)

Site of Forge

Modern Chapel

Gatehouse Bastion

(Shop)

Inner Bastions

Living Quarters

Entrance Bridge

Entrance to the Keep

Courtyard   Hall

GROUND FLOOR

Gunpowder Store

Well

'The Rounds'

Moat

Storerooms

Postern Gate

BASEMENT

N

0   50 Metres

0   150 Feet